Interior Design

A True Beginner's Guide to Decorating on a Budget

© **Copyright 2015 - All rights reserved.**

In no way is it legal to reproduce, duplicate, or transmit any part of this document in either electronic means or in printed format. Recording of this publication is strictly prohibited and any storage of this document is not allowed unless with written permission from the publisher. All rights reserved.

The information provided herein is stated to be truthful and consistent, in that any liability, in terms of inattention or otherwise, by any usage or abuse of any policies, processes, or directions contained within is the solitary and utter responsibility of the recipient reader. Under no circumstances will any legal responsibility or blame be held against the publisher for any reparation, damages, or monetary loss due to the information herein, either directly or indirectly.
Respective authors own all copyrights not held by the publisher.

Legal Notice:
This book is copyright protected. This is only for personal use. You cannot amend, distribute, sell, use, quote or paraphrase any part or the content within this book without the consent of the author or copyright owner. Legal action will be pursued if this is breached.

Disclaimer Notice:
Please note the information contained within this document is for educational and entertainment purposes only. Every attempt has been made to provide accurate, up to date and reliable complete information. No warranties of any kind are expressed or implied. Readers acknowledge that the author is not engaging in the rendering of legal, financial, medical or professional advice.

By reading this document, the reader agrees that under no circumstances are we responsible for any losses, direct or indirect, which are incurred as a result of the use of information contained within this document, including, but not limited to, —errors, omissions, or inaccuracies.

TABLE OF CONTENTS

Introduction 1

Basic Interior Design Principles You Need to Know 5

Use of Outside Space 15

Choosing Room Colors for Your Home 21

Keeping Home Makeovers Within Budget 33

Preparing Your Space For An Uplift 39

Knowing More About Different Interior Design Styles 45

Gathering Your Samples and Making a Design Clipboard 59

50 Interior Design Tips for Beginners 65

Simple Preparation Tips to Help You to Create Perfect Walls and Ceilings 85

Tips For Helping You Prepare Woodwork 89

Making Great Savings On Design Elements 91

Color Mixing and Matching Tips 95

Conclusion 101

INTRODUCTION

I want to thank you and congratulate you for downloading the book, "Interior Design: A True Beginner's Guide to Decorating on a Budget."

With a little imagination, you really can design the interior of your home to suit your own style. It doesn't always take spending a fortune. This book is geared toward those that want their homes to look designer style on a budget. Believe it or not, you really can improve what your home looks like by understanding basic design principles. Anyone can do it, with the knowhow that this book contains. It's put in an easy format so that you can use all the information to make your home as stylish as you can without spending an absolute fortune. Let's face it, with the way that money slips through your fingers these days, not a lot of people can afford designer style. They can, however, learn how to acquire it all on their own.

This is what this book aims to do. Stop complaining and start moving with easy to follow tips on how you can get started on decorating your dream home to your own specification. It's easier than you might imagine and cheaper too! The book is based on my experience as someone who likes to have a home that fits my style and certainly couldn't begin to afford professional help.

This book contains proven steps and strategies on how to decorate your home without breaking the bank. From interior design principles, to color psychology, and even tips on how and where to start, you're sure to learn everything you need to know about basic interior design in this book.

Thanks again for buying this book, I hope you enjoy it and that you will use the tips which have been gathered over years of personal experience and that these will help you to become very proud of your achievements as a homeowner. What are you getting for your money?

INTERIOR DESIGN

You are getting advice and lots of it gleaned from my own experience and this advice will help you put together a look that pleases.

The book explains different styles and what they consist of, so that you have a better chance of balancing the look. Interior designers have to go through years of learning, but people can also learn to watch as their homes evolve into the kind of spaces that they always dreamed they could have.

By understanding all the technicalities, the color mixes and the way that different elements are put together to create a look, you may be surprised to learn that you have all the makings of a designer home under your roof. All you need now is a little advice about how to put it all together because that's the trick that interior decorators know and that up until now you have only gleaned from photographs in magazines.

This book aims to put that right, by giving you oodles of ideas all in one place, so you can understand styling and how it works to fit your personality and your chosen style of living. Once you learn those techniques, it's unlikely that you will ever be satisfied living in chaos again. Switch your style – enjoy your own efforts and make your home every bit as inviting and enticing as those magazine pictures were. Once you know how, keeping it stylish is simple.

There are many ideas that you can use that don't cost a fortune as well, and it's always important to evaluate what you have and see how that fits into your chosen style. You never know, you may have all the makings of a great interior design style but just haven't discovered how to put that style together. When you do, your home will look beautiful and your guests will be delighted at your originality and all of the work that you put into making your home look as nice as it possibly can.

Of course, not everyone can afford top notch designer help because interior designer's services come at a price. However, when you know the rules yourself, you don't need them to help you. Mix your colors, change the styles of your existing furniture and add great artwork. If you have never designed a room before, this book takes you through all the stages so that what you end up with is a very stylish room, using established ideas that can fall within your budget.

If you're ready to take notes and learn all about what is learned every day in design school, then this book will be of great value to you, showing you images to demonstrate the styles talked about so that you can follow all the instructions easily.

BASIC INTERIOR DESIGN PRINCIPLES YOU NEED TO KNOW

Interior design is basically the method used for improving the overall experience of an interior space by those who live under that roof. Just by following some simple guidelines and honing in on your creativity, you can easily turn any space into your own style. Although it would probably take you years to become an interior design expert, knowing the following basic principles can help you keep on the right track. These are simplified so that you gain a great understanding of interior decorating principles as used by designers. These can be easily incorporated into the way that you view your home renovation or decorating project. Remember that these are only guidelines and you must choose what is relevant for your project from the suggested styles within this book.

The idea of sharing all of the different types of design is that you may not be aware of how interior designers work out what goes together to create a style. You will be given ideas on styling, colors and all kinds of tips so that even when you are working on a budget, you can make the most of what you have and minimize the fuss of a house that may have been built up over the course of years. One of the most important lessons that you can learn is to find a way to minimize all of those excess items which clutter your home. These are doing your style no favors at all. In a children's room, perhaps introducing more storage can help you to include styling even in their bedrooms, but remember that your guests see your kitchen and your living areas and dining area and that these are very important and present to visitors who you are.

Unity and Harmony
When designing the interiors of your home, you need to look at the whole house in its entirety. The design of each room should work in

unison with the overall feel of the home. Think of your home as a series of spaces being linked together by hallways and stairways. It's not advisable to decorate one room in one theme and decorate the others in a completely different theme. To get a cohesive look for your entire home, it's important that you have a common style or theme run through the different rooms. Interior designer elements should work together and complement the overall feel of your home.

The transition between one room and the next comes into the designer package. Supposing for example, you used clashing colors in adjoining rooms. It would look badly put together whenever the doors are open between the two rooms. This is why an overall style is chosen before you start.

That doesn't mean that you cannot use startling colors. Indeed you can, but the theme of these colors needs to coordinate so that what you see from one room does not look accidental when you gaze through a door toward another space. There are all kinds of ways that you can use continuation. Flooring, for example, should flow well. Breaking it up and having different flooring can really upset the flow of the rooms and people today tend to like styles that are more uniform in nature. For example, if you are going to have hardwood floors, it's a good idea to have them all facing in the same direction, rather than having parquet in one room and new flooring in another.

INTERIOR DESIGN

Image copyright: Houzz.com

In the above image, look how the old fashioned floorboard look as a great finish for rooms and hallway. What they have done here is polish up the old floors by hiring a sander and then staining them with a matt or satin finish without color added so that the natural color of the wood creates a great contrast to the white paintwork. If you wanted to make it look even more stunning, all you need are runner rugs in bright oriental colors and you really do have a stunning continuation from one area to another.

Balance

Balance can be best described as the equal distribution of visual interest in a room. There are 3 ways you can achieve balance in your interior design: asymmetrical, symmetrical and radial.

Symmetrical balance is more traditional and is considered to be the safest. You can achieve this effect by putting two of the same things on each side of the room. So if you have a nightstand on one side of a bed, symmetrical balance requires that you put the same on the other side. Symmetry is the easiest way to achieve balance in any room design. This could be achieved with artwork, ornament or even decoration. Two alcoves at either side of a fireplace can be balanced off nicely by decorating them in the same kind of colors, so that the focal point is the actual fireplace, but the symmetry of the room is maintained.

Asymmetrical balance on the other hand is more modern and lively. To achieve this effect, dissimilar objects are used to add visual weight to a room. So instead of adding another nightstand on the other side of the bed, you can maybe add a large mirror to achieve that sense of balance. The feel of this style is very casual, but it can get a bit too casual, especially if the design elements are not thought out properly. This form of decoration is very popular with young people who may have open plan spaces. By using this, the rules change and a wall of colorful wallpaper can be introduced to highlight an actual area of the room, rather than trying to balance the look by using the same décor.

Radial balance is achieved when elements are arranged around a central point. This is the least commonly used style since it requires a large space in order to be executed well. However, you can do this in a small room if you are clever about the content that you put into the room. For example, smaller furniture in a smaller room gives the impression that the room is larger.

INTERIOR DESIGN

Emphasis
Every well designed room needs to have at least one focal point. A focal point is that area in a room that doesn't just draw attention to it, but it should also create a lasting impression. In some homes, the focal point can be a fireplace, while in others, its windows. To create a natural focal point in your home, look for that area that is highly visible. Then place an interesting piece of furniture, or artwork that you want to highlight in that area. Make sure to maintain room balance so that your focal point doesn't end up hogging all the attention.

There is another way that you can establish which areas of rooms are currently the focal points. You may be disappointed to learn that the focal points that you are using actually highlight things you would prefer to hide. To establish what the current focal point is, close the door to a room. Then open the door and enter the room as if entering that room for the very first time. What is the first thing that your eye is drawn to? This is the current focal point but if you change that focal point, you can make a small room look larger, a dark room look lighter and a large room look more intimate and cozy. Focal point mirrors make a wonderful splash of light in rooms that are otherwise dark. A fireplace or a picture could be the focal point but they will only become the focal point if the arrangement of the room draws the eye toward them. If the fireplace is obscured by too much furniture or confusion, you may actually lose the benefit of it and instead, people will look toward other things within the room and that's a real designer mistake. Make sure that you are happy with the focal point within a room. In a bedroom, for example, it could be the bedhead. It could also be artwork on the wall above the bed. You decide what that focal point is and then work around it, making sure that the first thing people notice within that room is the point you want them to notice.

If you use too much busy furnishing or fill the room with too many things, you take away from the focal point and you need to remember the catchwords that less is more because it really is when it comes to focal points. However, when you are living open plan, you can create a focal point from the seating area toward the dining area to distract

INTERIOR DESIGN

the eye toward the dining area and to make a definite feature of that particular area of the room which is used for eating. This theoretically splits the area and gives a purpose to each part of the open plan room.

In the next chapter we will look at incorporating outside space so that your home becomes more spacious. In this day and age, this really is a possibility. Even the smallest of homes can be enlarged upon by full use of outdoor space at minimal cost.

Image: Houzz.com

INTERIOR DESIGN

In the above image, look how cleverly this household has used a bold image to draw attention to the open plan dining area making sure that guests can see the distinct areas of the room, even though it is open plan. It's quite a clever ploy to do this, and you may also wish to look at the lighting in the dining area and make it more subdued and intimate for those wonderful dinners with friends.

Rhythm

Rhythm in interior design refers to the design elements that lend visual interest through patterns or contrasts. It doesn't just add visual interest to a room, but it also makes it more interesting to look at. Think of it like telling a story. Your room should have surprising details to make it more appealing. If you want to show movement or rhythm in a room, you have 4 methods that you can use: repetition, transition, progression, and contrast.

Repetitionis when you use the same pattern, color, or texture in a space more than once. Using the same shade of yellow in your curtains to match a yellow rug in the same room is the perfect example of repetition. This is the easiest way to pull together the look of a room.

This is achieved by making yourself a design board. It may sound fancy, but it isn't. It's a clip board to which you add little pieces of potential fabric for curtains, photos of furniture which is of a set color that you can't change and paint colors to be used to go with all of those items. Having them together on a board allows you to cut out magazine snippets and ideas to give you the overall look within the repetition style, if this is what you want to achieve.

Transition on the other hand shows a much smoother flow. This method takes advantage of the viewer's natural eye movement and arranges design elements in a way that it allows the eyes to glide from one area to the next. An arched doorway or a winding path leads the eye to the next point of interest. This is why we mentioned earlier that it's so vital for adjoining rooms to be decorated in colors which go well together. When you open the door to the next room, the room can

INTERIOR DESIGN

be painted in a complimentary shade of the same color. This is cheap to achieve if you buy white paint and then use colored pigments to mix your own paints with. The colors that you achieve will be unique and you can keep a jam jar of each color as and when you finish a room, so that you have touch up paint if any is needed. Wear and tear can be kept to a minimum using this method.

Progression is when you use a design element in different sizes and color shades to decorate your space. Take for example a cluster of candles of different sizes to decorate your fireplace mantel, or using a monochromatic color scheme in different shades to make your room look more vibrant. The eye is drawn toward these progressions and from a bedroom through to a romantic bathroom, the ideas that you incorporate really can make a huge difference to how people perceive that space.

Contrast is bold and very straightforward. It's when you put together design elements that obviously oppose one another. The best example of this is using black and white throw pillows together on the couch, or using circle and square pillows together to liven up a space. Op art or opposite art colors were popular in the 1960s but have recently come back into style. Contrasting pillows, light fittings or ornaments use very bold colorings that contrast with the main wall colors.

Image: Houzz.com

In the above image, look how startlingly effective the design is, using black and white as the main colors for the scheme. You may not be able to afford designer chairs such as this, but you may still be able to create a room that uses contrast in every bit as an effective way. You may be able to buy, for example, a second hand table and paint it in matt black to have against white plastic chairs which are quite stylish but which don't cost a fortune. There are all kinds of ways that you create a look without spending a lot of money. Conversely, you could use other contrasts, such as red and white, blue and white, green and yellow etc. depending upon your preference. The idea is to make the room look stylish without overcrowding it with confusion.

Proportion and Scale

Proportion and scale go hand in hand because they both relate to the size of your design elements. You want your room to look just right - not too big or too small. Decorating a big room allows you to use larger pieces. If you're working with a small room, you should use design elements that aren't overpowering to the space. Many people make the mistake of trying to sell homes that are filled with clutter. What this does is give the buyers the impression that they have outgrown the space. That's what happens when you have a lot of items within a room. Thin down where possible, because less, in the field of home design, is often more.

By learning these design principles and how they go together, you'll be able to put together a room that you can be proud of. The next step is to add a bit of color into the mix. In the next chapter, you'll learn the basic psychology of color, and you can choose which colors to incorporate into your space as well as learning how to make up a design clipboard so that you can gather fabric colors, images and paint colors together to see what the end result is likely to be.

Look through style magazines or even look on Pinterest of Houzz, which will have loads of ideas. Houzz is particularly good because there are new things being added all the time and the whole website is devoted to interior decoration and style and you can pick up oodles of ideas without having to spend a lot. You may find that the furniture that you have is wonderful for mixing and matching, but that you haven't used it to its best advantage. Pinterest, on the other hand, is a website where you can pinpoint exactly which room you want to decorate and look at all the wonderful images that also give you many ideas. For example, using keywords such as "blue dining room" you will find that there are hundreds of photographs and that every shade of blue has been covered by people who pin their photographs there for members to enjoy. The thing is that you may be sitting on a very stylish sofa, but may not know how to dress it up to look stylish. The dining suite may also be a little dated, but it doesn't take much to bring it up to date.

All of these images are very much like looking through a style magazine and finding things that really do click with you. People have incorporated all kinds of ideas cheaply just by knowing the look that they are heading for and then adding the various elements into the right places that they already possess in other rooms. It's not a question of spending a fortune. It's a question of using what you have in many instances but in a more stylish manner.

Trying different elements of interior design in the room that you want to update will give you all kinds of looks and you can pick out which look suits your own individual style. Style is about making a statement about who you are. While organized people may be happy with a fairly minimal look, it doesn't mean that style has to be minimal. You are the only one that can make that choice and sometimes, you can cleverly use colors and contrasts to create a wonderfully stylish look from what you already possess. I know in one room that I had to design for a client, I actually saw the right elements in other rooms and asked her permission to experiment. What we ended up with cost her very little indeed because she only had to pay for fresh paint. The rest was gathered from other rooms and we were even able to stylize those rooms as we worked and she was very happy with the results.

USE OF OUTSIDE SPACE

How you use your outside space matters. If you have French doors to the yard, make the most of this by having these lead to an area where you can entertain outside. This expands your living space and makes it a great area to share with family and friends.

The important elements that will cost you money will be incorporating electricity because you will need lighting. It's worthwhile doing this because it's minimal cost gives you access to outdoor space even in the evenings. Building a patio doesn't have to cost you a lot of money. In fact if you collect broken paving from your local authority, often this is dumped and costs very little indeed because the local authority want to get rid of it. Making a crazy paving patio is so simple and although it requires a little bit of elbow work, will be well worth doing to give your outside space an actual grounding.

To lay a patio, you first have to dig out the foundations and use a lot of hardcore to give the patio something solid to be laid upon. This is relatively easy. Find all the rocks and stones around your yard and use broken bricks or rubble to give you the hardcore you need. This helps your concrete to have something to settle onto and should be covered by a layer of gravel and then sand. These products are inexpensive.

INTERIOR DESIGN

You can see from the above image that a patio does not have to be complex. As long as you make sure that you use a spirit level and that you take a slight slope away from the house so that rainwater is taken away from the property, you can make this any size you like, but as you lay each slab, you need to level it with the spirit level and bed each slab or stone into concrete. In the picture above, the homeowner is layout out the patio but this is a dry run. You can do this to get an idea of where everything goes first. Then mix your concrete and add it underneath your patio stones bedding each one in so that it is relatively flat and respects that slight slope away from the house.

I have done a patio from broken paving slabs that I picked up cheaply from the local council but have also done one with old bricks because these are very attractive. Pebbles are another possibility although flat stone is better and easier on your feet!

INTERIOR DESIGN

Look how cleverly this designer has made the outside space into another room. This book is all about interior design, but when you add a new dimension by making an outside space that follows on from your interior, it's every bit as important and can make your interior seem huge. Open doors to a patio which is furnished gives the impression of space and that's very important to making your home a really comfortable place to be. There are all kinds of budget furnishings available for an outside space and this means that your interior gains extra space and can look very attractive indeed. Even if you don't want to build a patio, decking does the same thing and doesn't cost a lot to install.

To maximize that outside space, make sure that there is a smooth transition from inside to outside and that you keep the doors open to encourage people to use that space. It's great for a drinks area for guests but it's also a very peaceful place to get close to nature and to sit a read a book, so your effort won't be wasted. In fact, you may even find that it frees up your interior space because people are automatically drawn to areas which give fresh air and sunshine. Be careful to have shade as well because summer days can be rather hot.

The kinds of things you can add to your exterior to make it part of the interior are colors which can take their lead from your decorative elements inside, cooking facilities, which draw people to the outside during the summer months, chairs that are comfortable for guests in the evenings and even loungers so that you can sunbathe. These are not expensive and for a minimum cost, you can open your whole living space up so that guests can see the advantages of the outside space that you have created.

You may even find that you can get second hand furniture which is ideal for this space but remember also that you will have to protect furniture from bad weather and may need to reserve a little space in the garage or cellar to house this furniture out of season. Add a few plant pots with luscious colors and you really can make this space an extension to your living room that invites guests outside where the seating area has been provided. More and more people are realizing the value of outside space and your interior will instantly look bigger if the outside space becomes a focal point.

Look at the simple construction of this furniture and you can see how you can create a seating area outside very easily. The boxes are dressed up with cushions which are easy to make in fabrics that you already have and you can use your backdrop as "walls" by adding artwork and other items of interest.

The outside space is exceptionally valuable and you don't have to spend a fortune to make it an exciting part of your living space, thus maximizing the potential of your home and making the transition between interior and exterior a natural one. Look for ideas in magazines. Gather bits and pieces from garage sales and bear in mind that when you open up your space in this manner, you make your living space seem a lot larger.

If you have the money to build a pergola that attaches to the house, this also gives you an element of protection from the weather and makes the outside area more inviting. Perhaps growing plants up the pergola can also make the area look very pretty indeed and there are a variety of plants which are suitable to use for this, including clematis, ivy, wisteria and many others that also give you color within the flowering seasons.

Doors to the outside space are vital. If your door is in the kitchen, for example, make that outside space an extension to the kitchen area by incorporating a table or picnic area where people are encouraged to eat outside. If the doors lead from the family room to the outside, use either a dining table for guests or have a seating area that is a natural extension to the family room and you will find that people naturally enjoy that space when the doors that separate those spaces are open in the summer months.

Your home may be small, but it can be made to feel a lot larger by maximizing on this kind of space. In some home, where you have a porch, make this the natural seating area and you find that people congregate there, freeing up internal space and allowing them to enjoy that extension to the living quarters of the house.

CHOOSING ROOM COLORS FOR YOUR HOME

One of the fastest ways to change the feel of your home is by incorporating color. Trends come and go, but color can give you that emotional attachment to your home. Use your design clipboard to gather samples of colors and fabrics as this will help you to be able to put effective colorings together. You only need a clipboard and can add many different elements to it to see how the colors work together. Small samples of background paint can be added, as well as digital photographs of wallpaper or furniture that you can't change, so that the overall scheme is pleasing to the eye and not confusing. Introducing too much bold color or too many variations of boldness can be very confusing and can spoil the style.

Picking the right color may seem daunting, but if you pull this off well, you'll end up with a home that you can be proud of. The trick is to choose colors that will help you achieve that effect that you're going for. There are different ways to pick out color but the best way is to choose colors that don't just look good together, but also give you the right feel for your room.

The first thing that you need to understand about picking color is that you need to think of the psychological aspect of colors. You need to pick out colors that will not only appeal to you but also be appropriate for the room. Color is one of the best ways to achieve harmony in your overall home design so make sure to choose wisely.

As a rule of thumb, lighter shades of color can make a room look bigger, while darker shades give it that sophisticated feel. So aside from picking out a color you like, make sure to choose colors that would match the room's purpose and the desired overall look. Here's a list of colors and the effect they can have on your home. Bear in mind that too much dark color may look overpowering and that if you want to incorporate a darker color into your color scheme you need to balance it off somehow. The best way that I know is to use the darker color for a feature wall or alcoves. This also helps you to economize because that way, if you want a stunning wallpaper, you can confine it to a smaller area as a feature and it can look stylish instead of overpowering as well as saving you a fortune.

Red

Red is a great choice if you want energy in a space. The warmness of red can draw people together and stimulate conversation. Although it may create a strong impression at first, you can offset this by incorporating neutrals in your color palette. Physically, red is known to raise blood pressure and heart rate so think twice before choosing this color for your bedroom. Red, however, would work perfectly for a living room or dining room space if you do a lot of entertaining.

If you examine the next photograph, you will note that the use of red was quite subtle and it added to the richness of the wood color of the furniture. This gives the room a traditional but well established classical look and that's what many new homes lack. Red can do that if you choose the shade of red carefully. I would personally use crown molding all the way around the room to give the room more consistency and would tend to use a lamp which incorporates the same red instead of a chandelier, but that's personal preference and you will have your own preferences.

INTERIOR DESIGN

In this room setting, the red chosen is subdued. What that does is give the home a richness without being overstated. It warms the room and makes it very welcoming and the home owner has used the coloring of the wall to reflect into the picture frames on the wall of the opposing color. That's clever incorporation of color. If you can't afford the frames you want, you can always paint up old ones and use them. A simple coat of undercoat and topcoat and you will get great results.

Yellow

Yellow is fun, vibrant and happy - perfect for spaces that need brightness like the kitchen or bathroom. Yellow can be energizing and uplifting so if you have any odd spaces in your home that need a bit of life, then yellow is definitely the color. But be warned. Yellow may not have a calming effect on some people. Studies show that people are more likely to get into an argument and babies tend to cry more in a yellow room. So if you're going to incorporate yellow into your color scheme, make sure that it isn't overpowering or avoid the nursery altogether. Pastel shades are okay in a nursery as these are not too overpowering for the baby and can also be the ideal choice if you don't know whether the baby is going to be a girl or a boy. In a case like this, instead of buying a special color for the nursery, why not buy white paint and mix your own color. It's cheaper and it's totally individual which means that no one else will have that exact shade.

Yellow in a kitchen can look rather nice, though pale yellows are preferred. These open up a space and make it look clean and crisp which is why pale yellow is often used for a wall coloring in a bathroom or kitchen. It is warm and welcoming and it's also a color that reflects light, so it's a good color to use to warm up a cool space in the home without taking away that element of white which is so important to the overall look of your home.

Image: Houzz.com

Look at how classic this yellow is and the way that the homeowner has incorporated stronger yellows in the upholstery and cushions, as well as adding accents of red to add a richness to the room. The transition from one room to the next is very subtle and looks very rich indeed.

Blue

Blue gives off a relaxing and serene feel, making it perfect for your bedrooms or any room that you want to have a peaceful feel. The downside, however, is that a blue room can make it seem uninviting and chilly, especially if you're going to use a dark blue shade. The results can be sad and depressing if you don't offset it with some warmer colors. If you want blue to have a calming effect on your room, choose brighter or softer tones like periwinkle or cerulean as your main room color. Blues work best in rooms that receive lots of natural light.

For smart contrast between colors, white works well with blue and gives the whole area a very clean feel. Look at the image below and you will see how blue can be introduced without actually being the main shade in the room, although it still retains its dominance over the style of the room.

INTERIOR DESIGN

Green

Green is the color that is considered to be the most restful for the eyes, making it perfect for your family room or living room. If you're looking for a color that combines calming blue and cheery yellow, then this is perfect for you. Green gives that perfect balance of cool and happy so you can use it as a main color for decorating just about any room. This color helps relieve stress and gives your room a fresh feeling so it would definitely work well in a home office.

If you go back to the times of William Morris and the Arts & Crafts movement, green was commonly used because of its links with nature. Some of the most stunning rooms use the arts and crafts paper to this day and still look wonderful. If you can't afford to do a whole room, why not have a panel? You can make one by buying a plain frame and simply wallpapering on a piece of card large enough to be placed within that frame.

Making panels to fit the walls of your home also gives you instant artwork at a fraction of the price, so you can make your home look stylish even on a stretched budget. I did this in one home and they really wanted the William Morris look from the Arts and Crafts era and how I did it was by making panels with simple wooden beading at the edges. Once the beading was stuck to the walls creating the panels, I was able to get away with using only one roll of the expensive wallpaper and it looked absolutely stunning and didn't give away the clue that we had skimped on expensive wallpaper because it went so well with the background color of the room and the furnishings within the room. William Morris came up with some stunning designs in all kinds of colors so they really are stylish to add to a room of any color at all and elements within the wallpaper can be picked out to get the exact match for the background color of the wall. In the photograph above, the exact match would be to use the paler color as it doesn't take away attention from the actual wallpaper itself. Had a darker color been used, it would have spoiled the look.

Purple

Purple is dramatic, rich and sophisticated, making it perfect for rooms that you want a lot of creativity in. The dark shades make great accent colors, while the lighter shades can bring a restful feel to the bedroom. Since purple isn't actually a go to color for many designers, you can use it to add impact to an otherwise drab room.

In the style shown below, purple is used to give the room a very grown up look and although used in small quantities, actually adds an awful lot to the ambiance of the bathroom, with the colors softened by painted floorboards and white backdrop to match with the stylized bathtub. None of the decorative elements used need to be that expensive but they do create a very expensive look. Even if your perfume bottles or shampoo bottles are only used as decoration, having bottles with purple liquid in them helps to keep the whole look in harmony.

Orange

Orange is all about excitement and energy so you can use this color for the kitchen or the living room. It will also look great in the kids' play area. Although it's not a very good idea for the bedroom, it can do wonders in your exercise space. The cheery energetic color might just be the thing you need to get through the most tiring exercise routine. Imagine the richness of color in a Moroccan home and you will also be able to see that mixed with dark red, it can actually make the room look warm even on a winter's day, but be sure that the furnishings that you use are not overly colorful as this will mean that you have too much color in the room and this can confuse the style.

INTERIOR DESIGN

Neutrals

To get the desired effect from your chosen colors, you also need to incorporate tried and tested neutrals into your palette. The great thing about choosing neutral colors is how flexible they can be. It allows you to use just about any color you want without coming off as too overpowering. You can add black, gray, brown, or white accents to tone down a strong red room, or liven up a dark blue room. Adding neutral colors into the mix can give your room much needed depth.

Neutrals also help with the flow from room to room because they create a backdrop and you can add your own artwork, rugs and cushions relatively inexpensively and make the rooms look an absolute delight.

Look at the colors in this room. They are such cool colors and what the designer did was use white as the main bed color and used a very subtle green neutral for the walls and the satin finish at the bottom of the bed. It looks super stylish and the cushions matched in the wall color so that the overall look is stunningly beautiful. It's also very practical because the seating area at the foot of the bed is so handy for dressing or for placing a dressing gown.

One neutral that cannot be over-emphasized in this day and age is white. It makes a real statement and looks so good in any situation. Add to that the color white is usually the cheapest you can buy and that makes great economic sense. The great thing about white is that you can add a few books, add rugs and a few really nice accents and you have an extremely stylish look. What's more, it's easy and it's not expensive, so the average home owner can use it to make their home look really great.

If you look at this image, the first thing that you see is the blue hydrangeas and the owner of this home has added another blue highlight in the colored bottles. Things like this don't cost money. You can find bottles at garage sales and pick the flowers from your garden.

The grey and white cushions add a little comfort to an otherwise very white room and the black accents on the furniture add a little more richness. In this image, I would have preferred to have seen artwork on the mantle, rather than having a TV screen but again, that's personal choice.

Now that you've got colors sorted out, it's time to start planning that room makeover. But before you go on a buying spree, learn how you can keep your interior design project within budget. The next chapter will teach you the budgeting tricks that interior designers are not telling you about. Why? Because they want you to employ them and use their ideas. However, not everyone has the money to employ interior designers and the tricks that are included in the next chapter really will help you to get off to a good start with your home design.

It's not as complex as you may imagine and the homes that you see in magazines really are not that difficult to achieve. It's a case of knowing how to blend colors, how to use fabrics and how to decide upon the colors of your home that will really help you. Sometimes obvious tricks really do work and this is where you will find this book handy because it's based on years of experience of renovating houses and making them saleable, by appealing to all kinds of different tastes.

If you think that interior designers buy everything new and thus you can't possibly keep up with the trends because of money constraints, think again. Many of the best interior designers that I know take inspiration from older items that are then used within an interior and which may be brought up to date with all kinds of painting techniques that are easy to master. The old established styles are very useful to create up to date looks as you can see from this photograph.

INTERIOR DESIGN

Interior design is something which evolves and by adding the right ingredients to suit your given style, you really can achieve this cheaply.

KEEPING HOME MAKEOVERS WITHIN BUDGET

Whether you're remodeling an old space, or decorating a new one, there are ways to get amazing design effects without breaking the bank. Here are some tried and tested tips on how you can update your space without spending too much. These are general ideas for many of the rooms of your house, but putting it all together will be a fun exercise and we will give you more details on this in a later chapter.

Go online

You can access great deals and great ideas just by going online. From auction sites to furniture outlets, the Internet can give you the lowdown on where to get the cheapest materials in your area. If you're lacking on creativity, you can get a bit of inspiration by checking out sites like Pinterest as we said in a previous chapter. Whenever you find yourself in doubt, just go online. One great site which gives you designs from all over the world is Houzz and on this website, you can collect images just like you would clip out pictures from magazines. These pictures are filled to brimming with ideas that you can incorporate without spending a lot of money. You may even be able to use existing furniture by sprucing it up a little.

It's worth having a good printer and printing out ideas because these can be added to your design clipboard and used later on. For example, you may see some really good matches in cushion covers and can make them at a fraction of the price. The idea is to keep ideas in your mind when you design a room and work out how you can incorporate these ideas into your planning of the home interior.

Check out garage sales

As they say, one person's garbage can be another's treasure. Don't hesitate to check out garage sales in your neighborhood to see what kind of furniture or home fixtures you can get for your design project. If there aren't any garage sales happening, then the next best thing would be your local antique shop. Although some pieces may cost a bit more, antique shops have unique and interesting pieces that you won't be able to find anywhere else. Once you find something you like, don't forget to bargain for it and never pay the price marked. Nothing compares to the feeling of saving a few dollars here and there.

I found some wonderful fabric at garage sales and also it's worth bearing in mind that drapes can be used to make cushion covers so never dismiss them. The fabric that they provide is ample for your needs sometimes and the color range available through garage sales may actually astound you. People tend to be faddy and when they change their décor, so too do they change their drapes and there's nothing wrong with the fabric. If you get lined ones, that's even better because often the lining can be used to create new and very stylish blinds for your windows to replace old fashioned curtains.

Visit wholesalers and outlet stores

If you want to get construction supplies like tiles, wallpaper or paint on the cheap, make sure to check out your local home outlet store for great deals. Ask to see discontinued items since these are often marked down dramatically. You can also check with wholesalers to see what materials you can get on a discount, especially if you're buying materials in bulk. Don't be afraid to ask about their return policy just in case you end up changing your mind about an item. I found some wonderful Moroccan tiles and because there were only a few, I constructed a panel in the center of white tiles and it looked super stylish. I added navy blue pencil tiles around the edge, so that what you saw looked like a designer panel. Adding one of these over the tub and another in the shower, the bathroom looked very stylish indeed but cost so little, because the white tiles I used for the majority of the bathroom were very cheap indeed, but the panels I incorporated took away that cheap look.

INTERIOR DESIGN

Something you can save money on is the items that a shop uses to demonstrate a style. If they have demo items, they often sell these when they change the décor in the shop and you can make some real savings. Look out for paints at all times, but always buy the best quality that you can afford as it will cover better and you will need less of it than you would if you bought cheap paint. You can look at kitchen suppliers and ask about ex demonstration kitchens. If they are updating their lines, it's quite possible that they have a whole kitchen out there at a reasonable price.

Check out cheaper alternatives

You don't have to splurge on materials to get the effect that you want so before you set your heart on that expensive printed wallpaper, do your research and check for cheaper alternatives. Don't blow off your whole budget just because you liked a specific fabric, or you can't do without those granite countertops. With countless choices out there, try not to settle for the first thing you see. Sometimes you can create a look without having to pay for the authenticity. If you can't afford designer wallpaper, why not limit the wallpaper to specific areas such as alcoves or panels. You will still be able to incorporate it, but you will use less of it.

Refresh fixtures

Instead of buying new fixtures, check if you can refresh them instead. Scratches on tubs and sinks can be remedied by a touch of paint or some polishing. You can also check online for service providers who can resurface kitchen and bathroom fixtures if you don't have time to do it on your own. There are cabinet paints which are great for your kitchen units and if your husband takes all the doors and drawer fronts out to the garage at the weekend, you could end up with a new looking kitchen next week. You can always buy new handles which are relatively inexpensive to give the newly painted items a fresh look. At the same time, this may encourage you to clean out all those cabinets.

INTERIOR DESIGN

Get into refurbishing

Why buy new furniture when you still have decent pieces you can incorporate in your design? Replace certain parts, smoothen out dings, and repaint dated furniture with new and exciting colors. With a bit of creativity, you can easily bring old furniture back to life. There are some great ideas for painting furniture on sites like Pinterest but be very careful that the furniture you are choosing to paint does not have an antique value, since some of this could be lost if you choose to paint it. Re-upholstery doesn't have to cost the earth. If you buy throws, these can be used to re-upholster a snug armchair and give it an up to date look.

Look at this makeover for an idea of space saving with modern design. It's simple little well thought out ideas that make a home look special and if you work on your designs on paper, you can come up with some great ideas.

INTERIOR DESIGN

Invest in good lighting fixtures

Strategic lighting is an inexpensive way to instantly change the feel of a room; so if you have money to spend, make sure to invest in good lighting fixtures. You can use a classy floor art to light up a dark area or if you have interesting wall art, use a spotlight to bring attention to that. You can also create an intimate relaxing setting by using low wattage light bulbs in your bedroom or living room.

DIY artwork

You don't need to spend a fortune to decorate those walls with precious artwork. If you want to bring attention to your drab walls, find inspiration and create your very own DIY artwork. A couple of large framed black and white family photographs would look gorgeous on your living room or bedroom wall.

If you are lost for inspiration, use Pinterest and you will find loads of ideas that you can create yourself from nature. Creating your own artwork actually adds to the style of the interior because no one else has those pieces of art that you are so proud of.

Work with what you have

For someone on a tight budget, the best fixtures and home accessories are those that you already have at home. Before spending money on new fabric or linen, make sure to do an inventory of home items that you can use in your design. You'll never know what kind of interesting home accessories you already have lying around.

I used to have a collection of fabrics that was intended for a quilt that I never got around to making. I was able to incorporate the colors into my new design and did this in a subtle way. The fabrics were so decorative, they gave the room more style as they were used for cushions and to match off with those cushions, I used samples of the fabric in frames with a cardboard vignette and they looked very attractive.

INTERIOR DESIGN

Never say no to second hand frames. They are always useful and you can always paint them to suit your interior décor. In fact, I have a great collection and simply change the artwork, when they begin to look a little tired. You can also color the frames each time, so that the look is fresh and clean.

I find that hardwood floors are great too, because with the addition of an occasional rug, you can enrich the colors within a room and make it look really tasteful. Sometimes, you have many items that you put away in the loft or the cellar and you can refurbish them to make new items to go into your design. Never be too proud to upcycle. It's a great way to get new items for your rooms. Old furniture items can be painted to fit in with your style and those old tired upholstered seats can be re-upholstered very easily. All you need to do is remove the fabric and use it as a pattern for your new fabric. It's as easy as that. If the upholstery under the fabric is solid, then this is a good indication that it's only the fabric that needs changing.

PREPARING YOUR SPACE FOR AN UPLIFT

When you assess a room that you want to update, you need to see the actual measurements on paper and also see what it looks like empty. Often, you have so many items in a room that it obscures what you could actually do with that room. If it's at all possible, try to empty the room so that you can have a good look at the shape of the room and decide from there exactly what you want to do with it. It's always easier to work within a room that has been cleared out. Even if this means placing the furniture into the garage for the time being, you get a better shot at designing your room in a more efficient way if it's empty.

Drawing out the dimensions of a room
If you can treat yourself to a booklet with graph paper, drawing out the dimensions of the room gives you a better idea of what you have to play with. For example, you need to mark out where the windows are, where you have fixtures which cannot be moved, where you need any electrical work done, since this would need to be done before the decoration stages. Planning your space helps you to save money long term because you are able to see exactly what you have and buy or refurbish items which will make the room look more modern and updated without flooding the place with items that are too large.

Mark the measurements of the room onto the plan, so that you know how wide the window openings are, where radiators are placed as these cannot be moved and will constrict what furniture you can place in the room. Mark doorways.

INTERIOR DESIGN

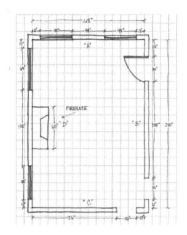

As you can see, the measurements are important and help you to plan out your room. You are also less likely to make errors if you know the room dimensions. I remember one friend buying a combination sofa and finding that she couldn't get it into the room! Measurements are key to interior design. They also help you to understand your space better and to maximize it.

Natural light

The natural light within a room is vital to how the room looks. You may have had old fashioned drapes which do not pull back entirely to the rebate edge which means that you may actually be losing natural light. In this day and age, it's a great look to let the light shine into the room. Perhaps you can replace old heavy drapes with linens which allow that light to shine through. Lightweight linen curtains come in all different colors and are reasonably cheap to buy these days, so you may find that you can update the look of the windows and give yourself all the light that you need at the same time. Alternatives could be linen curtains made from lining fabric, which is always going to be cheaper, but which will also let the light get into the room.

By maximizing the light that flows into a room, you actually create a wonderful atmosphere because outside light makes the room look larger and you will see things much more clearly. Imagine your newly decorated room flooded with daylight and you will see how essential this is to good design.

Flooring

If you have not updated a room for a long time, you may find that the flooring that you are using is very outdated. Many people who remove old carpet find that underneath that carpet is a wealth of history. Great floor boards which were thought of as unfashionable in the past are in vogue big time. If you find that you have wooden floorboards, it really won't cost you a fortune to do them up so that you have a finished floor. The hire of a sander and a bit of work and you can make the flooring look pretty good. The imperfections that you find are part of that flooring add character, so don't be too worried about them. If you use oriental style rugs on wooden flooring, these look superb.

Hiring a professional sander is better than using your own because it's likely to have all the attachments that collect the dust. This is essential because, believe me, you will create a great deal of dust during the sanding process and if you can minimize it, all the better. The industrial sanders work on a larger area as well meaning that you cut down the amount of time needed to sand the boards. Always sand in the direction of the grain of the wood and you end up with wonderful floors that look like they have been freshly installed.

If, however, you do need to replace the floor covering and are working on a particularly tight budget, there are options. You could make the whole room look lighter and airier by having a light colored flooring and laminate may be worth considering. If you do consider laminate, don't go for the lowest price as this won't be good quality. If you look for prices mid-range, you can get some great bargains and they are so easy to lay yourself. However, for a child's bedroom or guest room, you may want to consider the linoleum which is available today as it is cushioned for comfort, easy to lay and can give you a really nice surface which is easy to keep clean.

If you are giving a bathroom an uplift, then because of the relatively small area you are working with, it may be better to use tile because this is easier to clean. It won't cost a lot because the square footage of a bathroom is likely to be relatively small. If you are going to tile a floor, you need to work out how to deal with the transition from the tiled floor back out into the hallway and the bars that you can buy which fit tiles on one side and wooden floors on the other may be the best option. You will also need to lay a subfloor in hardwood because if there are floorboards, there is too much movement to lay tile effectively and the tile will eventually crack with the movement of the boards.

Looking at your lighting

If the lighting in the room is not making your space look nice, you can of course change shades, but what about getting recessed lighting? This relatively cheap form of lighting is worth considering because it gives such great light which can be adjusted to suit the moment. Thus with dimmer switching and recessed lights, the room takes on a whole new look.

It's important to look at all alterations which are going to be made to the electrical installations within a room before considering decorating it. While the room is empty is the ideal time to assess this and to have an electrician give you a quotation for this type of work. It may be cheaper than you may imagine and it's always worth talking to the electrician about different possibilities as some alterations will be cheaper than others. He knows where the wiring for that room comes from and will thus have a better idea of what he can do without it costing you too much.

Taking off old wall coverings

This may look like a daunting task but taking off wallpaper is not as hard as you may imagine. With the room empty, you do need to cover the floors to protect them from any dampness and also from slipping on wet wallpaper. For this task, you will need a bucket of warm soapy water, a sponge and a scraper. If your wallpaper is vinyl finished, there is a tool that you can use to grate the surface of the paper so that the water that you sponge onto the paper goes right through all layers. Ask at your hardware store as this is a very inexpensive item and you will use it a lot. After having scraped the surface of the paper, soak an area with soapy water and allow the water to penetrate. If you try removing the paper too soon, you will find it tough going, but if you wait long enough, this will peel off very easily. If one area isn't ready to peel yet, work on another area, adding water so that you work in a rotation.

When peeling off old wallpaper, some of it will come away in large chunks. Have waste disposal bags available and place these easy pieces into the bag straight away. In fact, when you peel paper, get used to binning the paper as you work, so that you do not cause areas to become slippery under where your steps have to stand.

You will find that the paper removes fairly easily, but that there will be little bits left behind. This is normal. When you have finished the whole room, go back over the walls with a clean damp cloth and use your scraper to remove these. They will become yellow when wet and you should be able to see them clearly. The reason it's so important to remove all of the little bits is that they will show through whatever new wall covering you choose to use in the room.

Sugar soaping the paintwork

This is all part of the preparation process and doesn't take long. The paintwork including the architrave around a door, the base boards and the windows will all need to be washed down so that the years of dirt of dust is removed ready for rubbing down the surface for paint. Sugar soap is semi abrasive and helps to give you a really clean start, so that when you work on the paintwork, it will look as if performed by a professional. That saves you money and gets you good results.

The room is now prepared and you need to decide upon the style that you want to create in that room. In the following chapter, there are some details which may help you to decide upon an interior decorating style that is suited to your room. Look through the ideas and also look up images on Pinterest or in magazines that give you an idea of what you can do with that room. You'd be surprised at the results you can get without having to pay professionals to do the work for you. It just takes patience and knowing what to look for.

KNOWING MORE ABOUT DIFFERENT INTERIOR DESIGN STYLES

If you're starting an interior design project, one of the first questions that you need to ask yourself is, "what style should I choose?" It doesn't matter if you're decorating a condominium unit, or a 3 bedroomed house, picking out a specific style can make decorating a lot easier.

If you want to be able to put together a well-designed room, you need to consider 3 things before picking out a specific style. First, it should look well with the rest of the house, second, it should be appropriate for the space, and third, it should reflect your personality and taste. Don't be afraid to mix and match different styles if you're going for a unique and vibrant feel. To get started, here are just a few interior design styles that you can draw inspiration from.

Modern

The modern style is great for smaller homes like apartments because it's functional and maximizes space. Colors are kept in the neutral color palette, with maybe one bold color as an accent. Function always comes before form so you'll see a lot of asymmetrical balance in the room.

You can tell that a room is done in the modern style when you see a lot of clean lines and minimal use of textures. This style provides a simple and calming feel to a room. This kind of style is suited to any room at all but if you use modern design, remember that you can still have features or focal points within a room and that won't take away from the modern look.

In fact, if you have great artwork, even if it's home done, it can look wonderful on plain walls. Use matt paints because these are non-reflective and much calmer on the eyes. It is also a good idea from the point of view of hiding any defects. Matt paint tends to do that very efficiently, whereas anything with a sheen will immediately highlight badly prepared areas.

As you get to know your home from a decorating stance, you will also know the areas which need to be hidden or which need extra preparation. It's worthwhile to do that extra preparation, but there are paints that can help you to disguise badly cracked walls and to make them look like new again. Get accustomed to learning the difference between different interior fillers because some shrink and need two coats whereas others do the trick first time. That's worth noting because it saves you so much time during the decorating process at a later date.

Look how the modern lines are used in this bathroom. The bathroom is still very functional but not fussy or busy. That means that decorative elements are kept to a minimum and that the overall look is a clean one. Towels can be blended in with the color of tiling if that's something you want to incorporate and the style of faucets used is simple and unfussy. It's also very easy to keep clean. Glass is becoming more and more popular, but you must use the correct type of glass that is strengthened and is intended to be used for shower areas. This is a safety element so if you have to splash out on anything within the bathroom, make it the glass. The tiling is something that you can do. Look out for vanity basins in stores that offer discounts as sometimes you can get some pretty modern ones at minimal cost but do make sure that all the faucets and parts to put it all together are included in the deal. In the above image, they have used a non-slip surface in the shower and this is another safety feature you could incorporate.

Contemporary

The contemporary aesthetic gives off a trendy welcoming feel, making it perfect for people who like to be in style. Colors and furnishings are basic and bare, but bold at the same time. Open space is an important element to this style, so clutter and extra details are absolute no-nos. Geometric patterns and unique furniture pieces are used to add interest to this style.

This kind of styling is popular today for living spaces because it affords individuality and it doesn't cost the earth to create a space that is contemporary in style.

For example, you can have individual artwork items that give it boldness and these don't have to be expensive. It's where you place things and the colors that you choose that help to pull this style off.

INTERIOR DESIGN

You could hunt out contemporary items in an antique or second hand store and you may even possess contemporary seating but have not really been able to see it because the room was too busy with other things. Look how the single chair in this picture stands out because the background is minimalistic and the contrasting colors used are plain.

The seating that you can find in garage sales may also be very useful to this style. Do you remember the picture of the contemporary dining room earlier in the book? It used plastic chairs and used the contrast between black and white and you can get away with all kinds of color combinations.

Urban

Urban interiors are perfect for those who want to combine living and working spaces together. This is a style that is often seen in converted buildings like renovated warehouses or studio apartments. Making use of open wide spaces, the urban style showcases creative use for exposed structural materials. You'll also see a lot of industrial materials like steel pipes and refurbished pallets used as furnishings. Creativity is key if you want to pull off that urban feel for your multifunctional space.

This kind of style is usually divided into separate living areas, not by walls but by clever placement of furnishings and by the decorative elements that are used so that those different areas can be distinguished, one from another. For example, a dining space within an urban interior may be colored in a different way and have different lighting to the general living space. This adds focal interest to an area within a large space and makes it feel more intimate.

This is the kind of style that would be used in loft apartment, but in homes that are open plan, it works perfectly because it allows the homeowner to show off those areas that have been set apart for dining, living and for play areas. This makes it particularly family friendly.

Classical

Classical design is based on symmetry and balance and is heavily influenced by classic Greek and Roman design. One thing that really defines the classical style is the use of a focal point in the room such as a fireplace or a large piece of furniture like a piano. Furniture and decor are then arranged around the focal point to highlight it. Natural colors and textures are preferred in this style to give it a warm feel. Fabrics used are more traditional, adding to the room's overall elegance.

Classical styling may also be that style of decoration which is in character with the era in which the building was constructed. Many people like to bring a home back to how it would have been originally presented, as fashions have changed over the years. Stripping back the layers of superficial decoration can often give very pleasing results because many of the classic features have been hidden because of changes in fashion. However, truly classic style will never really go out of vogue.

Wood is high on the classic interior style image, but nowadays wood can be painted to make it lighter on the eye and to give your interior a great boost of light.

INTERIOR DESIGN

The tradition of fireplaces and shelving actually can look very smart indeed and you may have alcoves that you can use to add all that extra storage space without having to buy expensive furniture but instead, using built in items. If you have too much wood and want to minimize the look because it's too overpowering, you can do that by painting it white, but be prepared to rub it down well to help the paint to go on smoothly. You need to rub it down between every coat and you may find that using a satin finish will make it hardwearing but also very calming. The above image shows how wooden cabinets can look when they are painted white and it's still classic, even though you have brought it right up to date with your paintwork.

Outdated fireplaces are something that you can easily update as well. There are wonderful finishes now to cover over those horrible bricks or you can paint them, but make sure that the paint you use is suitable for a fireplace. If you have a real fireplace with a grate, of course you can't update what it looks like in the grate area very much but you can tidy it up. I had one fireplace which was badly burned. I managed to get fire bricks which were really thin and managed to do a herringbone pattern to cover the blackness. I then invested in a second hand fire back so that it couldn't happen again. Herringbone looks so nice and I didn't want it going black like it had before.

Art Deco

Art deco is generally sleek, with touches of drama in furniture and decor pieces. The feel is very glamorous with lots of industrial metals and lacquered wood accents. To add to its dramatic feel, black or a darker shade of purple is used as the main color. In order to counteract the dark feel of the color palette, table lamps with frosted shades can be used. This design is known for being intentionally overly decorated with bold colorful wall art, bronze accessories, and etched glass vases.

If you like Art deco, then think angles because it's usually the angles that give away this styling. Think dramatic. Think theatrical.

INTERIOR DESIGN

You may even be able to find pieces that are suitable to this style in second hand stores and they may just be the pieces that make the difference between bland styling and definitive Art deco. Look at the clever tiling in this image and you will see that they contrasted black and white tiles and that the tiles were nothing spectacular but the design was drawn out for the tiling so that what it created was an Art Deco finish that went in with all the extra bits and pieces added to the bathroom.

Retro

When old trends make a comeback, it's often with a modern twist. This style may be difficult to recognize at first look, but if you see classic pieces and colors that remind you of a specific era, then you'll know it's retro. Whether you're going for 50s Americana or 70s disco, make sure to use materials and artwork that are reminiscent of the time. To keep the look modern and up to date, try not to saturate the space with too many nostalgia pieces.

The retro look brings back old type styling in cookers or refrigerators and colors that are pastel blended with other colors such as used in the tiling in this image.

This kind of style can be something from your past or from TV shows that are in the retro style. If you think of the television series of the Fonz, this is the type of dateline that you are aiming for with furniture in the style used at that time and light fittings which are retro as well.

Retro is really stylish. People love those old fridges and cookers and if you can find them in good condition, you really can make a room look very stylish indeed. You may even discover some retro style in the garage of an old aunt or your parents' house. People tend to tuck these away for utility use in garages because they were made to last much more so than the units of today.

Country

If there were two words to describe the country style, those two words would be cozy and homey. Think cottage living in the countryside. Rich in nature inspired and floral patterns, this style gives off that warm, comfortable feel, with the tendency to become cluttered with all the bulky wood furniture. But even though it may look and feel dated, the textured walls and the unfinished wooden pieces give this style that rustic feel.

Country styling is quite easy to reproduce without having to spend too much. For example, the colors that you choose for your painting can make all of the difference to the way the room is presented. A rustic country style would typically use colors that are warm, earth tones so that the overall impression that people get when they look at the interior of the house is warmth and comfort.

Artwork can help here as well. If you choose small print wallpaper for a guest bedroom, you can use artwork which has a plain border and which matches in with the colors on the wallpaper. If you want to make savings, use wallpaper on the wall where the bed head goes and paint the other walls in plain colors that match in with the wallpaper. You can actually get tubes of color that you mix with paints and make your designer paints much cheaper than actually buying the exact color in the shop.

Minimalist

The minimalist style originated from the concept of Zen philosophy. It simplifies living spaces so that you end up with an open organized area. The sense of order adds to the visual interest of this style. Cool colors are used with white to give it that clean feel. The minimalist style is often used in large spaces and uses only a few essential furniture pieces. Natural light in this setting is used as a feature and is highlighted in the choice of minimal decor.

One of the features of this style of interior is that there isn't any clutter. Things have their place and everything is put away so that the overall look is uniform and neat. Minimalistic styling is easy to keep clean because the style positively encourages tidiness. If you like this style, it's unlikely that you would be someone who likes clutter anyway. Essential to this style is good storage so that you can have as many possessions, but don't need to be constantly surrounded by them.

Victorian

If there was a style that was the complete opposite of minimalism, it would be Victorian. This style is flamboyant, luxurious and excessive with the decorations. But even though it might feel like there's a lot going on, it doesn't look cluttered. The Victorian style color palette mixes deep hues with pastels and neutrals, serving as the perfect backdrop for the heavy wood furniture. Walls and floors are kept bare as much as possible in order to contrast the decorative features of the style.

The Victorian era was one when decoration was beginning to flourish in the interior of a home. Pictures were extravagant in presentation. There was also an elegance about the furnishings which were used and you can recreate this style using second hand furniture which can be used to dictate the color scheme used. Window seats were a popular theme in Victorian houses since many had bay windows and cushions were certainly popular.

Georgian

The Georgian style is characterized by elaborately carved furniture and luxurious fabrics. The color palette of this style may be particularly pale, but the rich mahogany furniture makes up for it. Patterns and colors of the drapes are subtle with hints of Chinese designs in the prints. You'll also find Chinese porcelain lamps and cabriole legs as pleasant decorative surprises. The fireplace is often the heart of the room so more often than not, furniture is arranged to achieve radial balance.

In the Georgian era, people were a little more extravagant with their interiors, but these days you can reproduce that look relatively cheaply. Cornices, for example, were in vogue and so were chair rails. These can be installed these days relatively cheaply since the cornices are made of polystyrene rather than plaster, and a homeowner can easily install them without a great deal of expertise. Chair rails were useful not only for the function of protecting the wall from the chairs being rubbed against them, but also as a decorative element since you can decorate above and below chair rail level with different colors to get even more visual interest or to make a tall room look more in proportion.

Rococo

This interior design aesthetic features a lot of intricate and ornate details found in its decor and furniture pieces. Rococo is rich and flamboyant and isn't apologetic about it. You'll also see a lot of gold painted furnishings contrast with the subtle pastel walls. Curves and spirals are dominant design elements, giving rococo style a hint of playfulness. You'll find multiple large mirrors on the walls, as well as expensive ornately framed paintings of people or landscapes.

INTERIOR DESIGN

Rococo is easy to imitate because there are so many variations of this style and you can pick up a lot of items that fit into the style of your room from reclamation yards or from second hand stores.

By now, you probably already have a good idea on how you can decorate your home in the style you want. But before you get started, don't forget to read up on the last chapter on interior design tips, especially written for beginners as well as familiarizing yourself with techniques which are shown in the chapters that lie ahead.

Creating a style means getting the room ready for that style and then creating a design clipboard, collecting all the ideas that you can, ready to use to create the style you have chosen. The furniture that you own will place you under pressure because you may not be able to afford to replace it. Thus, try and go with the style of your furniture. It's a good idea to minimize the amount of furniture that you have built up over the years and put some of it away because this makes the rooms that are about to be remodeled look bigger. Often families build up a load of excess furniture until rooms look cluttered. Introducing your furniture a few bits at a time you will get to feel when you have added too much.

Collect color samples, collect fabric samples, but remember that everything you do to that room must go with upholstered items that you cannot afford to change or that those items will need to be updated by using throws to disguise the color a little. That gives you a little more flexibility in styling and isn't at all expensive to pull off. I remember in one home, I had horrid green sofas. I had inherited them when I bought the house and couldn't afford to replace them. I bought several throws and stitched these as upholstery over the top of the existing upholstery and added a pleated hem. They went well with oriental style rugs and looked very classy but the truth was that they cost me very little to update.

INTERIOR DESIGN

Sometimes you have to be bit inventive and looking at what other people have done can give you some great ideas of your own. If you room is tall, for example, make it look more manageable by learning all about how color affects a room's presentation. If you paint the upper section of a wall in one color and then introduce a chair rail, you can use another color below the chair rail and give the impression of less height.

Your clipboard should be filled to brimming with ideas and when it is, you really will know the direction that you are heading in and can look out for bargains that help you to create the style that you have in your mind.

GATHERING YOUR SAMPLES AND MAKING A DESIGN CLIPBOARD

Now that you have an idea of the style that you are looking for, do browse through magazines for ideas and clip out any pictures that you think will help you in your search for the perfect style.

You need a clipboard with your plan attached to it and the things that you need to start seeking are ideas that you want to put into practice within that space. You will first need to decide upon the color palette that you will use for the room as this is vital to your choice of fabrics and accessories and paint colors, as well as ornament and wallpaper.

If you have items which are upholstered, then you will need to take digital photos of these if you know that the upholstery is not something that you are going to change. Often you have to work with what you have and use the main colors of items which will not change to balance with any new colors that you introduce to the room.

For example, you may have a dark blue armchair, but that doesn't mean your whole room has to be blue. You have to choose clever color schemes which blend with the blue rather than make the whole area blue. Look at the image below and you will see what is meant by this. In fact, very little about the room in question is blue.

INTERIOR DESIGN

The designer of this room has cleverly incorporated neutral colors and then used the blue chairs as a highlight which is balanced out wonderfully with the picture windows. Yes, there are little touches of blue in the decoration, such as on the table, though the overall color scheme is not blue per se. Thus, you can pick colors which blend nicely with the upholstered items that you have and take samples of colored fabric and paints to try and bring the whole look together.

The paint colors will be important, but it's the overall look that matters. As you add a fabric or a color stand back and look at the overall balance of the look and decide whether your choices are good choices or nor. You can mix patterns, but be careful how you do this as if you have too much pattern, this can distract the eye from the overall design. A design board is basically a collection of ideas that you want to put together. You can add to it or take away from it but at the end of the day, what you are looking for is perfect balance to suit the style that you are trying to create and it doesn't always take spending a lot of money to create a wonderful style.

INTERIOR DESIGN

In the above image, the designer has put together different fabrics and color swatches together with ideas from magazines and this is the kind of thing that you are trying to create. See the groups of fabrics. The designer is grouping items, which means that not all of them need be used, but by moving around the swatches, it gives the designer a better idea of what would work well together and what won't. That's important.

The fabrics may be used for cushions or something like that and the basic colors of your room may be fairly bland. These cushions can add zest to the room and a lot of great interest when someone looks at a room. The big plus with adding cushions is that the amount of fabric that you need to create them is a relatively small amount so that this kind of décor does not have to cost a great deal.

You would be surprised which colors work together. Gone are the days when people don't mix certain colors. In fact, some of the most stunning interiors that I have seen have really gone against the old rules of not mixing earth colors with blues. That idea has long since been dismissed and people are learning to mix whatever is pleasing to the eye.

Gather swatches as these are free in fabric shops, gather wallpaper samples as these are also free and in one case, I got some wallpaper samples which were actually large enough to put into artwork frames with a nice cardboard around them that made them look extremely stylish without having to spend all that money on wallpaper I couldn't afford.

You can try almost anything. Remember the basic rules that dark colors close an area in and that light colors make a room look larger. Of course, you can have that bright red wallpaper if you want it, but limit it so that where you place it is minimal but still gets all the attention that you intended. If you do a whole room in red, you will be very lucky to get away with it because it tends to close the room off and make it look very stifling. Remember that the colors you choose are something that you are going to have to live with and that's very important. Can you see yourself getting up and relaxing in that room if you paint it with dark purple? Although fads come and go, don't risk an error like that, because you will inevitably have to redecorate the whole place to get rid of it and dark colors take a lot of covering!

It may even be worthwhile trying a small area of paint because paints don't look the same color in the can as they do on the walls. I tend to mix my own colors because I know exactly what I am getting, but you can also mix bought paints with coloring to make them a little more unique. When you see the paint in the room that you are about to decorate, the light will have an effect on how it appears, so use a small board and paint it and place it into the room in question to see if the color matches that color you intended to introduce. It it's not quite right, you can always add a touch of colorant to get it to the exact color you envisaged.

In fact, this is a great trick for making your paints match the color of your furnishings. I always take photographs of sofas and things that I can't change and take these to the shops so that I have them available to check out colors that may go well with them.

Get loads of color cards. These are usually free of charge and they let you adjust your thoughts when you put your design clipboard together as one subtle change of tone can make all the difference to the color being used. When you do check out colors of fabrics against the colors of paints, be sure to look at them in good light as often shop light gives the wrong impression. I have been known to take cushions to the window of the shop so that I can see the exact colors and photograph them. Shop owners can be very helpful and provide swatches of fabric that a sofa is made of if you are going to make that kind of purchase and this will help your design clipboard tremendously.

When you gather samples together, don't be afraid of mixing different patterns. Although it may have been frowned upon in the old days, today you have a lot more flexibility as mix and match is one of the tricks of decorating that designers use to give a room more interest. Focal points are important and these should have colors that you can add as accents elsewhere in the room. That focal point, for example, may be a portrait that you already own. Look at the colors within the portrait. If you close your eyes and then open them to look at your picture, you can get a better feel for what the overall color is. The strongest color in the picture will always be the one that you see as soon as you open your eyes.

Pick this color up in candles, vases, baskets or small items that don't cost a lot and you have a coordinated look. I find that candles are very popular these days and having them in glass containers means that you see the full color of the candle and can use this to match with objects that you have as focal points.

The trick is not to overdo it. Crowded rooms do not make very nice areas to live in. The way to get over this is to add your accents a little bit at a time and when you are satisfied with the overall look, don't add anything else to the room. Overdoing it always looks overstated and people will question your design if it is cluttered and think that you didn't put much thought into it. It's far better to have less than more and to add to it, rather than too much.

50 INTERIOR DESIGN TIPS FOR BEGINNERS

Whether you're decorating just one room, or your entire home, creating the perfect space can be a fulfilling experience. It shouldn't just be pleasing to the eye, your space should represent who you are, and at the same time serve its purpose in your home. If you've always wanted a home that you can be proud of, start with these foolproof interior design tips, especially put together for beginners.

Tip 1 – Color schemes

Pick out happy colors for rooms that you regularly use for entertaining. Bright colors are awesome for stimulating conversation. They are also colors which will catch the light and make the room look warm. Happy colors are all the natural colors and if you are a little frightened of being too bold, stick to using bolder colors in smaller areas, using more subtle shades in areas which are larger. You can always add artwork to walls which are bland and use the feature color for the picture frames, thus bringing harmony to the whole look.

There are more details on color schemes in other chapters, but remember the rule that warm colors are happy colors and may be the best choice for family rooms, so that the room gives off an air of peace and calmness that you and the family can enjoy, with the odd splash of color intended to make a bold statement.

Tip 2 – Pieces that fit your space

Before investing in a chandelier, make sure that it works with the room not just style-wise, but proportion-wise as well. You don't want the piece overwhelming the room. This isn't just with chandeliers. This also means when you buy any item to fit a room. For example, if you have a small guest room and fit a large double bed, it will automatically shrink the space. Try a three quarter size bed and it instantly makes the room look bigger.

Size is important because it means proportion. If you have a small wall and hang a huge picture, it's okay as a focal point, but if you were to do that on all the walls, it would look out of proportion to the room. Thus, before investing in anything which is size detailed, think out your space and know that the size is correct for the space in which the item will be placed. This is a really important part of design. Look through house magazines and look how things are always put in proportion to room spaces. If you break that rule, it will look obvious and won't give the aesthetically pleasing appearance that you want the room to give.

Tip 3 – Buy chairs and table separately

Looking for a new dining set? Find chairs that will look great with the table. Pay attention to scale and make sure that the seat height is compatible with the table height. You may be able to find bargains in an antique or second hand furniture store, but do be sure to try the table and chairs together before parting with your money. Similarly, furniture stores may have items that can be bought separately which you like. Place the items together before making the purchase and do try the chairs for comfort with the table.

As you saw in a previous chapter, white and black go together so well and if you buy separate chairs and table, you really can tailor make the look of your dining area. It's the modern way of being individual and for some reason, it works.

Tip 4 – Careful choice of lighting

Lighting can make or break your space. If you want to get it just right, check how your rooms look with natural light and try to replicate that. If you want to create two separate spaces within a room, that can be achieved by having focused lighting in the dining area of the room which hangs just above the table and thus draws attention to that area.

INTERIOR DESIGN

This is great for when you have guests and need not cost a fortune. The lighting in a child's bedroom should be practical. Perhaps the child will not be too keen on the darkness. Thus, use a bedside lamp which is themed for a child and as the child grows, you can simply update the lamp.

In a kitchen area, why not have lights that are sunk into the ceiling and don't require cleaning? They are much more practical and can be placed over the island area so that you have loads of light for preparation of food.

Bathroom lighting should be relaxing. This is an important room for seeing yourself as well. If you can use subdued lighting for the bathing area, you could also have spotlighting for near the mirror so that you have adequate light for makeup or for shaving.

Tip 5 – Use of illumination

Light your favorite things in a room rather than just the space. Don't just use lighting to brighten up a room; use it to show off your personality. For example, if you have artwork or ornament that cries out for lighting, then this doesn't have to be expensive, but can look very chic indeed. If you have a favorite set of glassware, having this on shelves which are illuminated lets the light reflect from the glass and can look very attractive indeed.

INTERIOR DESIGN

The lighting used on this picture is first rate, because what it does is help to show off the artwork and the home designer has added pottery to go with the color of the painting so that the overall look is very warm indeed. This small additional lamp isn't expensive but it's certainly worth thinking about if you want to show off items as a feature in a room.

Tip 6 – Use muted colors

Muted walls, floors, and sofas act as the perfect canvas for any room design. Invest in classic pieces and colors and indulge in trendy items like pillows and lampshades as these will add great interest value. Rugs are also an addition which adds richness. Sometimes, you can get away with bland coloring on the overall design if you bring in accessories which show off the room to perfection.

INTERIOR DESIGN

Tip 7 – Using pieces with historic interest

If you want to add interest to a room, incorporate one item from a different era and showcase it as the room's show piece. This could be a rocking chair in front of a fireplace. It could be a blanket box at the end of a bed or a four poster bed. Having something of historic value really does add to the way that the room is seen by people and you may just want to use items passed down through the family. An alternative is to find items at garage sales and spruce them up and use them as center pieces, because there certainly are bargains to be had.

If you don't have heirloom pieces, then why not paint a piece of furniture as a center piece. Sometimes, that newly painted item can really set the room off and look very interesting indeed. You can even try your hand at different finishes since there is so much special effect paint on offer these days that's it's easy to create a masterpiece for the fraction of the price that one would cost you, had you bought it already finished to your requirements.

Tip 8 – Golds, silvers and metallic colors

When utilized tastefully, metallic shades like gold and silver can add a luxurious feel to any room. These can be used sparingly in a dining room to blend with the colors of the edges of your porcelain, or used in a child's room to give an ultra-modern feel. Perhaps the best place for metallic is in a computer room where you want to create a space age environment and this can look very good as well as helping keep dust at bay. A desk with a metallic worktop or a wall behind the computer in metal can look fantastic.

Even the incorporation of metal in a kitchen helps to give the kitchen clean lines. Some of the world's most famous kitchens incorporate stainless steel worktops and these can look stunning. If you cannot afford them, then you can add utensils to the kitchen on racks so that they are seen as part of the overall picture.

INTERIOR DESIGN

Tip 9 – The rule of threes

Always decorate in threes. Hanging family photos on the wall? Hang three! Placing throw pillows on your couch? Do it in threes. Decorative elements in threes just look more polished. This could equally apply to candles on the dining table or the mantle. This is a great look and even three vases with separate flowers in them placed on a dresser can look more stunning than a single vase.

Tip 10 – The addition of rugs

A statement rug in your chosen color palette can really help put together the look of a room. It doesn't just add a splash of color, it can also be functional and give the room a warmer look. When choosing rugs, if you can't afford the authentic, look on websites such as eBay because you may be able to afford more rug than you thought possible. Rugs add a huge value to a room and also give the room a feeling of comfort.

Tip 11 – Use mirrors wisely

Mirrors should be a staple in your room design. Mix and match different shapes and sizes to create a dramatic focal wall. The other reason that mirrors are so important to design is that they instantly create more light in a room especially if they are placed to reflect window light. They thus make the space look larger than it is and that's a great tip for those who have small homes and want the big home feel.

Tip 12 – Family photos

Pick out your most favorite photographs and have them framed. Turn a blank and boring wall into your very own memory gallery. This is a great area to have in any room but the family room and the hallway come to mind. Hallways are usually fairly bland and a gallery of family photographs up the stairway can look stunningly beautiful, if you choose the right frames and make the look very intentional rather than merely an accidental gathering of images. Colors and styles of frames will help to draw the gallery look together.

Tip 13 – Buy quality

Designer branded furniture pieces aren't always well made or comfortable. If you're going to invest in expensive furniture, make sure to choose a piece that will last you a lifetime. You can often find wonderful furniture in second hand or antique markets but don't part with your money too easily. You may just get it at a price which you decide upon rather than paying the price on the ticket. Auctions are another good place to find furniture which other people don't want any more but be sure to examine the piece thoroughly before you place your bids.

INTERIOR DESIGN

Tip 14 – Invest in artwork

A few key pieces of artwork can really spruce up your home so invest in a few that you really love. Move them around from time to time to give rooms a whole new look. Artwork is value because it means that your home looks more polished and finished. If you cannot afford originals, then prints are just as good, but you do need to have these framed nicely so that they don't look cheap. The presentation of pictures is everything. Give them a head start by choosing frames which really do complement the style that you are trying to create.

Tip 15 – Add period drama

If you have architectural details built in your home like dramatic stairways and hallways, highlight these features with well-planned lighting. These are parts of the past but they are probably what endeared you to the place when you bought it. Highlight them and let that historical look come out. Fireplaces which have been hidden behind drywall for years may be stunningly beautiful and can be featured as a focal point in a room. Old cornicing painted looks wonderful and can give character to a room.

Tip 16 – Plump up the cushions

You can never have too many cushions in your home. Purchase them in bulk to get a good deal and use your design board to look at all the fabrics together. If you can't get samples, photograph the fabric and look at them from a short distance to see which colors work best together. In a shop situation, lay the chosen cushions out together and see what the overall effect is. Cushions are a cheap investment. They add color and style to a room without having to spend a great deal of money, but without them, a room can look bland and uninteresting.

Tip 17 – De-clutter

Whenever you feel like your space is starting to get cluttered, take a moment to purge items that just don't belong in the overall look of the room. You simply can't showcase a room well if there's clutter everywhere. That is one of the reasons that we suggest you empty a room before you decorate or remodel it. This gives you the bare bones of the room and you can introduce pieces one at a time after the decoration is done, deciding which pieces would be better elsewhere. If it doesn't add to the style of the room, it doesn't belong there.

Tip 18 – Keep window treatments simple

Keep window treatment for big beautiful windows simple and elegant. Always make sure that you have enough sunlight coming in during daytime. To see how much light you could be getting pull the drapes away from the window recess and watch how the light transforms a room. Heavy, overstated drapes can kill a good design and make it look old fashioned. It's much more fashionable to use linens that allow the light to pass through into the room.

Tip 19 – Color tips

When deciding on your color palette, always make sure to add a couple of neutrals into it. No matter how bold your chosen colors are, your color palette is guaranteed to stay elegant if there's at least one neutral. This may look boring on its own but what happens is that you use feature colors on small walls, for example, and use the neutrals for ceiling and the other walls. Then bring the look together with artwork, photographs or decoration which actually brings the featured color onto the neutral wall tastefully. Remember, don't overdo it.

INTERIOR DESIGN

Look at how neutral the color scheme is in the above picture. The designer has used the yellow painted furniture and picked up the color in the flowers in the room. Bright colors have been introduced, but the basic backdrop of the design is a neutral color which really gives the whole space light.

Tip 20 – Make your home a treasure trove

Display only what you love. Anything less would just be a waste of space. If that means finding new homes for things which are perhaps functional rather than decorative, then that's the best way to deal with items that don't do the room justice.

INTERIOR DESIGN

Tip 21 – Move things around

To see a room's full potential, don't be afraid to rearrange furniture every once in a while. This will help you see things from a different perspective. Therefore, it's not a good idea to have too much fixed furniture which doesn't allow you this pleasure.

Tip 22 – Update furniture

Have an old piece of furniture that you can't part with? Update it with new fabric. It's a quick fix that will instantly update its look. Before you do this, make sure that the furniture is not valuable as this may actually lose you money, but if it's simply shabby and needs to be chic, then upholstery is the way to go. This can be done easily to dining chairs, armchairs and even sofas. When you take off the old upholstery, use the pieces that are removed carefully as your pattern for new fabric, but don't buy fabric which is not intended for upholstery as it won't last long.

Tip 23 – Use shapes that enhance your space

For smaller rooms, choose round tables so that space flows better. Minimize hard edges if you want a room to look more spacious.

Tip 24 – Simple and functional

If you have a limited budget for furniture, make sure that you invest in simple and functional pieces. Resist the urge to splurge on embellished furniture as these can be hard to mix and match. Simplicity of furniture style means that you get to decide what the overall look is all about rather than letting fussy furniture dictate to you what it should go with.

Tip 25 – Change the handles

Change up furniture hardware with some statement pieces. The extra bling can glam up boring furniture. Knobs and knockers are relatively cheap and you can get some great looks from a small investment, using your existing furniture but giving it new fixtures and fittings.

INTERIOR DESIGN

Tip 26 – Colors for a warmer room

When choosing colors for rooms with natural light, go for jewel tones. This will really brighten up the space. It also makes the room look warmer. White may be the preference, but white in a large space with good light can actually look cold.

Tip 27 – Buy sufficient materials

Always make sure that you have all your materials before starting a job. Create a list of your needs for the preparation of the room, for the painting and for the additional touches. Stay within your budget. If buying wallpaper, make sure that all rolls have the same dye lot because if they do not, you will see a slight variation in color. It's better to order one roll too many than not enough.

Tip 28 – Use your design clipboard

It helps to have a color scheme ready before you get started on decorating a room. It helps you stay focused on the look that you want to achieve. That's why we insisted that you create a design clipboard. This way the look that you end up with is not accidental, but completely planned to look great. It's worth taking the extra time to do this as the end result will look more professional.

Tip 29 – Look for natural inspiration

Draw inspiration from nature and art instead of trends. You'll never go wrong with nature inspired tones and designs. Look for inspiration in magazines and you will see that natural art really does look comfortable when in place, rather than trendy art which may look dated within a short space of time. Nature is never out of fashion.

Tip 30 – If in doubt, leave it out

If you have doubts about a certain pattern, just move on. You have to either love it or hate it, and there is no in-between. The point is that you will be looking at those designs every day and if you don't have enthusiasm for them on the first day, imagine what it will feel like when you have to see those designs daily. Don't compromise. Neutral paint and a picture looks better than walls done in a color or style that you are not sure about.

Tip 31 – Add textures

Add depth and interest to a room by using different textures. A room that looks too polished can come off as boring and unwelcoming. For example, you can introduce textured cushions, rugs or even wall hangings at a relatively small cost and these add real wealth to a room's design.

Tip 32 – Ceiling colors

Try painting your ceiling in a light shade of your room's color. This will help make the room taller and airy. If you have sloping ceilings, you can paint these the same color as the wall to give the room unity.

Tip 33 – Using neutrals

If you're still unsure of the colors you want to use in a room, always start off with neutral walls. Starting off with a blank slate allows you to add whatever pattern and color you want later on. If you are a little afraid of a color, you can always make your base coat lighter than intended and build this up on the final coat.

Tip 34 – Paint bold pieces

You can up cycle an old table or chair by painting it in a bold color. This can be the perfect project for you if you're looking to change up your furniture without spending much. If you are nervous about being that bold, choose an item for the room and paint that. This could be a chair for a child's bedroom or a dresser for a guest bedroom. Give yourself time to get confident with painting. Remember that you can always repaint it if you are unhappy with the results.

INTERIOR DESIGN

Tip 35 – Using color to calm

Desperate for a good night's sleep? Use pale shades of color for your bedroom. This way, you won't feel stimulated before bedtime. Lighting is also important. If you can have dimmer switches, these don't cost a lot and you can turn the light down to relax your eyes, with bedside lamps for reading so that you have the choice.

Tip 36 – Layering the look

Keep your color palette simple and just add drama by layering your room with different materials, textures, and lighting. Try not to play it too safe, when it comes to picking out decor for your room but if you need to gain more confidence, that color can be added to your design board first, so that you can get a good idea of how the different colors will go together when the room is painted.

Tip 37 – Add vibrancy

Have a lot of vibrant pieces and patterns that you want to incorporate in your design? Then keep walls and window treatment subtle. This will help keep the room looking classy, with that element of fun. Remember the importance of focal points as these vibrant pieces really can make a style statement.

Tip 38 – Try prints

Don't be afraid to play around with prints. To maintain the room's look, choose different prints in different shades of the same color. This can be for your upholstery, cushions, drapes and wall hangings. Printed fabrics can be very attractive.

Tip 39 – Opposing textures

Opposing texture can create a stylish contrast for your space. Utilize it well. Look at this mixture of cushions and you will see what is meant by that. You don't have to be boring in your style. Add colors and patterns with panache.

INTERIOR DESIGN

It is the overall color that will always shine through, but look how colors were used in this design. They cleverly verge upon a rust color and give an overall impression of harmony. Add the flowers for softness and you have a stylish look that didn't take a lot of effort to create.

Tip 40 – Use of grey

Grey may not look like an exciting color, but adding it to your bold color palette can generate a very interesting look for your room. It's the best color to build your color palette on if you like softer colors. White is very stark and grey gives you a little more softness which can be added to with colors such as blue, yellow, pink and even green. If you are mixing your own paints, keep a stock of black coloring because it flattens a color and makes it very suitable to add with grey. The kind of colors that use grey are duck egg blue or a very nice pastel green. If you add it to pink, you actually take off the girly look and create a very grown up pink that's suitable for any room. Black coloring is great for making your colors original.

Tip 41 – Design and color for class

If you want to create a comfortable and livable space, combine a subdued color palette with a symmetrical room arrangement. It's the easiest way to create harmony in your design. Colors from nature give a warm look so you can plumb for beige and different subtle shades of green or yellow blending each room with the adjoining room by changing color slightly but keeping it within the same range of colors.

Tip 42 – Use artwork for inspiration

Find inspiration in your favorite artwork. You can easily build a look for the room by taking note of color shades and details that are used in the artwork. If this is a favorite piece and you use that as a guideline, you won't go too far wrong in creating a look around that artwork, rather than fitting the artwork into a particular style.

Tip 43 – Calm the ceilings

Use matt paints on ceilings as these are non-reflective and can create a calm environment much more easily than using high gloss finishes. In fact, high gloss can make a room look big and impersonal as well as showing up all the flaws in your walls or ceilings. Gloss or satin is also quite cold and matt paints for ceilings mean that people who enter the room will notice your wall decoration more because it discreetly sits in the background and doesn't distract the eye.

Tip 44 – Use of florals

Floral elements can liven up a space instantly. Make sure you have at least one floral piece in a room. If you can't bring yourself to use floral wallpaper, then simply having artwork or a vase with flowers that can add warmth to the design. Even in a bathroom a single stemmed flower can look stunning, especially if the color is bold such as in the case of roses, blue flowers or even yellow sunflowers.

INTERIOR DESIGN

Tip 45 – Mix new with old

Don't be afraid to mix old with the new, bold with the simple when it comes to buying pieces for your room. Often this works well as modern and old go well together to create an overall individual style. If you have a classic dining area, why not incorporate lighting which is old fashioned such as chandeliers which are popular in this day and age, as well as having a great table cover. This doesn't have to be the old fashioned style of tablecloth. It can use delicate lace as a runner or something that adds a little more richness to the room and that blends with other colors used within that room. You may even be able to match napkins to that central table decoration and that always looks good.

Tip 46 – Creating interest

Line the back of your bookcases with your favorite printed wallpaper. It doesn't just add color to the space, it also adds depth. If you are not keen on this idea, arrange your bookcases so that they are filled to brimming with books of similar sizes and the color of the books is arranged so that it looks wonderful and adds a rich layer to the room. White bookcases with a whole heap of colorful books looks very stylish indeed and saves you having to add much more color to the room because the books provide enough on their own. Bookends which are stylish are inexpensive but can look great against a white background.

Tip 47 – Dark colors

If you're going to use dark colored paint, make sure that it has a sheen finish. Flat dark paint will only make your room look depressing and boring. The best finish for this kind of paint is eggshell which is subtle and satin rather than shiny and too bold. When using this in dark colors, make sure that you walls are prepared correctly before painting because every flaw will show. If you are using wallpaper, you still need to prepare your walls to a perfect flatness as dark colors tend to show up so many flaws that you may not have been otherwise aware of.

Tip 48 – Natural light

When choosing colors, make sure that you check how they look under 2 kinds of light. Natural and artificial. If you use your clipboard, you can examine this easily in daylight and if you are taking photos of existing furniture, try to take these in good light so that the colors are as accurate as possible. Natural light within a room should always be maximized because it's softer than light that is introduced and flattering to the room as well as giving it a sense of warmth and space.

Tip 49 – Accent colors

Repeating accent colors in your pillows, linens, or floor rugs in different rooms can help connect the whole house together. Don't overdo it, but it can give the home great harmony. It's that feeling of transition and smooth transition from one space to another means that people see your home as well planned and designed, rather than accidentally having the same style.

Tip 50 – avoid op-art

Following a black and white scheme may seem easy enough to pull off, but it can get boring really fast. Add texture to prevent the look from coming off as flat. Break the monotonous feel with the use of flower arrangements, layered fabric and natural wood furniture. Black and white dining suites are very popular at the moment and if you feel that you want to incorporate one, make sure that the other colors within the room compliment it, rather than having everything in monotones. You can introduce reds to a table top, or a wonderful display of colorful glass bottles. Your lights can be colored so that the black and white doesn't give that coldness that it's known for.

All of the tips and tricks that are included in this chapter have been tried and tested and are based on experience. You can be experimental

INTERIOR DESIGN

within the parameters of sensibility, but these tips will help you not to make design mistakes that you will regret. Remember, if you working on a budget, mistakes cost money, so it's better to plan things out before you execute them or before you shell out the cash to invest in items that really don't give your home the style you intended.

Even small items such as cushions can cost a fortune, so mix and match them in the shop so that you know what they are like together before taking them home. When you make your own, you save a lot of money and matching fabrics is sometimes easier for those who have no experience of design. It's easy to see flat fabric and to place the fabrics together to see if they work well. Stand at a distance to judge because this gives you the chance to see how the fabrics blend and you can replace a fabric that you don't feel does any justice to the design.

The home gives you so many opportunities to exercise your own sense of styling. Remember that simple designs such as white can be made to look stunning if you have a lot of possessions that are colorful and you want to draw attention to them. Sometimes simple designs work better than complex ones and keeping to white in a case like this makes good sense.

Draw up ideas from different cultures as sometimes a Moroccan interior can be warm and inviting, or a Chinese style interior be organized and have clean lines. Whatever you incorporate into your home has to be the backdrop to your family life so go with practical but also remember that style is easy to emulate by being observant and reading a lot of house magazines that give lot of ideas that will really help you in your design decisions.

I cut out pictures all the time because it's important to me to keep gathering up ideas for future use. They may not be of use straight away, but if you they appeal to you, cut them out and keep them safe because one day, you may find them ideal to your design process, even if this is years from now.

SIMPLE PREPARATION TIPS TO HELP YOU TO CREATE PERFECT WALLS AND CEILINGS

Although people underestimate the importance of the preparation, it's more important or at least equally important as the finish because you will see if walls and ceilings have not been prepared correctly. Since you are working on a budget, chances are that you are undertaking the work yourself and this may be the first time that you have tackled it. The information below should help you to see how to prepare walls and ceilings so that you get great looks.

Tools required for preparation:

- Paint Scrapers in various sizes
- Interior filler or spackle
- Medium and fine grain sandpaper
- Drop cloths
- Stepladder
- Dust brush

Before you begin to prepare your walls and ceilings, you need to protect the floor beneath where you are working. This is vital because you will create a lot of dust.

Place the drop cloth onto the floor and don't be tempted to use polythene as this is too slippery and your ladder may slip. Cloths which are of decoration quality are the best, but if you don't have these, use old sheets.

Examination of the surfaces

You will need to examine the surfaces of your walls and ceilings to find all of the cracks. These are quite normal in any home. Likely places that they will occur are at the junction between the wall and the ceiling, between the wall and the baseboard and corners of a room. In all cases, you need to scrape out the crack to remove loose debris. Even if the crack looks small, rake it out using the side of the scraper to create a "V" ready to take the new filler.

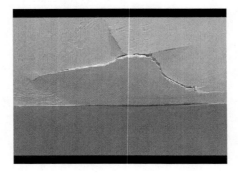

If you see cracks like this, don't be too worried. Part of the crack is hollow and needs to come down. If you tap it, this will begin to remove it. Bear in mind when you are dealing with cracks such as this, you will need to clean out the surface and brush it before applying plaster and will need to build up a layer of filler at a time, rather than trying to use too much in one hit. Let a small layer dry and then add another as this is much more likely to give you great results.

In the case of hairline cracks, scrape out the crack, sweep it with the dust brush to get rid of loose debris and then fill, using your paint scraper flat against the surface so that the filler goes into the crack but you don't leave excessive amounts of filler as you pull the paint scraper or spackle knife over the surface.

Allow this to dry. This is very important. Before you are able to apply paint to the surface, you need to rub this down with medium and then fine sandpaper so that the surface is completely flat. If you do notice that it needs more filler, then it's more prudent to add this than to ignore the problem hoping that the paint will cover it. It won't.

After the filling has been done and you have sanded down all the areas which have been filled, use a sweeping brush to brush down the walls so that all the dirt is removed from them before paint is applied.

Where baseboard and wall meet

This is always a difficult area, since the baseboard may come away from the wall at any time and it always looks unsightly when there is a gap between the baseboard and the wall. If you are sure that the baseboard is sufficiently fixed to the wall, then you need to use your paint scraper or spackle knife to apply filler between the baseboard and the wall. If you use a dampened cloth what you can do after you have filled the entire strip is run your finger along the top of the filling protected by the cloth, to take off any excess filler and to give you a perfectly smooth finish ready for rubbing down and painting, once it is dry.

The preparation of your surfaces cannot be over emphasized in importance. This gives you a chance to look at the structure of your home and to notice if there are reasons why areas are cracking or whether there are stains appearing on the surface of a ceiling. The reasons may be simple to rectify and may even have been rectified in the past. For example, a leaky seal around a shower or bathtub in the room above may just have meant that water was leaking onto the ceiling.

To get rid of stains on ceilings

The most effective way to hide these unsightly stains is to use an oil based undercoat just on the area which is stained, before you paint the ceiling. This must be given sufficient time to dry.

If you find that the stain still needs more coverage, try a little more undercoat but be patient as this process will be worth your while at the end of the day, because it means your new surface will not be ruined by having the stain seep through your new paint.

TIPS FOR HELPING YOU PREPARE WOODWORK

It's vital to remember that even though the springtime sunshine may have arrived, wooden surfaces can contain moisture from the winter and if you paint too early what you do is trap that moisture into the wood. Wood should always be painted at dry times so that the dampness within the wood is given time to dry out before you even start preparation.

Windows

If you have windows to paint, you will need to check putties, especially on older properties that don't have double-glazing. Putty is what keeps the glass in place and if it is cracked and worn, it's better to remove it and to re-putty. This may sound complex but it's a whole lot easier than trying to paint cracked putty and get a good result. If you can remove the window and place it onto a flat surface, this helps. Carefully chip away at the old putty and make sure that the glass surface is clean ready to take fresh putty.

Often you have to work putty between your hands so that it is pliable and easy to apply. This is applied with a putty knife but before you do that, you put the putty in place with your fingers so that it fills the edge that is missing its putty. When you have done this, the knife is dragged across the putty to leave a straight line. Don't worry too much about putty getting onto the clean window at this stage. Let the putty harden before you consider painting it.

If you really can't do this job yourself, you may find a jobbing builder who is able to do this part of the decoration on a fairly tight budget as it doesn't cost as much as redecoration, but is worth doing properly.

When you paint windows, you need to have them fully prepared. That means cleaning them down, opening the window to clean out the frame and using sandpaper to rub down the surface of the wood. If there are cracks, you will need to use a filler which is specifically manufactured for exterior work, even if the window repair is on the inside. Wooden windows are exposed to the weather and therefore exterior grade filler is the only way to go.

MAKING GREAT SAVINGS ON DESIGN ELEMENTS

The idea of this book is to give you a lot of detail so that you can use this to help in your experience, though this chapter helps you to create you individual style but save money at the same time. We have gone through all the rooms of the house and given you tips as where savings can potentially be made. Remember that all electrical work and plumbing work should always be done by a qualified person who can ensure that the work is done to code. It's important that this is respected so don't try to make savings in these areas as it may be a false economy. The money that you save elsewhere in your design elements will free up more money to help you to use the professionals when appropriate.

Entrance way

This is the first area that people see when they enter your home. Make it bright and airy and a great transition to the rooms that go beyond it. In this area, you can save money by buying paints during sales and making sure that you buy white as your predominant color. Then, add color tubes so that you can mix your own colors. That means that you can create a great color for the entry way and then carry on in the same scheme of color but changing the shade a little for each of the rooms that transitions from the hall.

Family room

This is a room where good planning will help you to make savings. For example, MDF built in cupboards to house all of your entertainment items will be cheap to make and you can paint it to match in with the walls so that it doesn't look out of place. MDF is easy to work with and you can get some great plans for making units or simply work on your own design, buying sufficient MDF to make all the units you need for

DVDs, CDs and the actual TV and accessories, so that they are neatly put away and don't depend upon independent furniture items. In fact, built in, they blend into your design in a much better way.

The artwork in the family room can be something you can make. If you like a particular wallpaper but don't want the cost of a dozen rolls, use a frieze and create oblong shapes on your walls and paper within the oblong. It's stunning, it's cost effective and means you can have those designs in your room without splashing out too much.

Dining room

For this area, try to find pieces that go well together in antique stores. A great table doesn't have to cost the earth and chairs which are comfortable with it are also something you can pick up relatively cheaply. The dining room can have additions such as candles to give it atmosphere and if you don't want to spend a fortune on lamps, look at standard lamps in antique stores and simply change the shade to give a whole new look to them. These create ambiance in a dining room area and you won't have to pay extra for the electrician to wire in new lighting.

Kitchen

Use cabinet paint on your cabinet doors, after degreasing them and rubbing them down. There are paints which are specifically made for cabinets and they are worth the investment because they are made to take the bumps that kitchen cabinets will be subjected to by normal wear and tear. You can clean up the handles or even buy new ones at a fraction of the cost of new cabinets and if any of your hinges have dropped, buy new ones and affix them at the same time as you decorate and they will look as good as new.

Tiling in the kitchen often gets marks in the grout lines which look unsightly. You can actually buy tile paint which covers the whole area and can be wiped, so this may be an option. Otherwise, what about cleaning the joints with either a steam cleaning nozzle or by using specific products to get them back to looking great again. If all else fails, you can always use an artist's paintbrush and paint the joints with an oil based matt finish so that they look spotless.

The nursery

An old cot or crib can look every bit as good as a new one if you paint it up with baby friendly paints and add a picture to them. To do this, simply source a picture you like and trace it onto the furniture, painting it with baby friendly paints to give the crib a really up to date look. You can make mobiles which hang above the crib and paint walls in light colors that are calming. An old rocking chair painted in pastel shades could be placed in the room for the nursing mom and the whole room will look newly designed and welcoming.

Children's bedrooms

Let the kids help in the artwork. Why not have a wall devoted to them, using lining paper and old picture frames, so that the kids can draw in the picture frames and create their very own look? You can save an awful lot of money on furniture for kid's rooms by painting up second hand furniture, but be careful not to skimp on things like the mattress since there may be hygiene concerns.

Guest bedroom

Here, be inventive. Imagine yourself staying at your house. Make the room welcoming, but look out at garage sales because you might just find the treasure of a quilt which will give you great guidance in your choice of colors. Wall hangings are another thing you may consider as these can give you real design ideas for the room itself, based on the general colors of the items that you have purchased.

Bathroom

Look for tiles which are end of stock but do make sure that you buy sufficient for your bathroom. Buying a few square meters more is better than simply scrimping and buying exact because you will have breakages during the tiling process, but huge savings can be made by choosing end of lines.

COLOR MIXING AND MATCHING TIPS

If you are able to get yourself a set of tubes of colorant, you can save a fortune when mixing your own colors and they will be totally individual to you. That's a great saving and individuality sorted out. So how do you get the right colors? Mixing paints is a little bit of an art, but generally packets of color will come with a guide as to how much paint is mixed to achieve a certain color. The trouble with this method is that it depends upon you to stir your paints well and to only put a little bit of color stain into the paint until you are happy with the results. Adding the colorant a little at a time is always the wise way to go. Remember that adding it to water based paints, the color will need to be a little darker in the pot than your intended finish because emulsion paints dry lighter. However, if you are using colorants in oil based paints, be gentle with your mixing as they take less colorant and will quickly color up, making it easy to make mistakes.

The stock colors that you need to have are as follows:

- Raw Sienna
- Yellow Ochre
- Black
- Whichever shade of blue you like
- Red
- Whichever shade of green you like

The main reason for having black as a standard colorant is because this helps you to make a bright color a little more subdued. I use the black in pale green and blue to create duck egg blue and ice green as the black helps the color to become a little paler and more like the colors used in an Art Nouveau style interior. These colors are very subtle and look very good on the walls and are a little less obvious than the colors you can buy directly off the shelf in DIY stores.

With the above colors in your toolbox you have the possibility to create any color but you may have forgotten the recipes for mixing colors.

Red and Yellow = Orange

Red and white = Pink

Red and Blue = Mauve

Green and Blue = Brown

Blue and Yellow = Green

However, there are variations. If you mix blue and yellow but have primarily blue, you end up with turquoise. If you mix red and yellow but make yellow the principle color, you end up with peach.

Picking out bold colors
Within a room where you want to make a real statement with accent colors, you can use those accent colors to color the baseboards within that room. These look particularly stylish.

INTERIOR DESIGN

In the above image, the accent color chosen was lime green. It's not everyone's cup of tea but look at how it fits with the basket in the unit. By doing this, you bring a little more detail into a room. White baseboards are classic and give a great finish to a classic interior, but you don't have to stick to white. If you have a newly tiled kitchen in very dark tiles, as is the fashion at this time, why not color your baseboards the same color as the tile, so that they look like they go in with the tile? It looks stylish and it suits the room without drawing the eye down to baseboards in standard white that break up the styling of the room.

Mixing and Matching
You can get away with all kinds of color mixes these days but you would be wise to use color cards to see which colors blend well with

fabrics or to see which color creates what impression. Look at the images below and you will see what I mean.

In this image, you wouldn't normally put this kind of turquoise with blue walls, but they have cleverly made sure that everything ties in my use of the blue in the cushions. The white panels on the wall fit with the furniture.

When you want to try new experiments with color use your design clipboard and see how they all go together. If you can find a shade that helps them all to be harmonious, it can work really well. For example, cushions used to be all one uniform color. Now look how they are used and you will see that colors are mixed and even the patterns can be blended and it still looks super.

INTERIOR DESIGN

Even the most unexpected of color schemes work, when you blend colors with other areas within the room. In this instance, the wonderful warm peachy color blends with the gray as if the two colors were made for each other and the cushions match the table covering. You could even add artwork with a touch of both colors and it wouldn't be overdoing it.

When you want to mix colors, you may even want to try out drawing the room and adding the colors in watercolor so that you can see the effect before you actually paint your room. A lot of interior designers use sketches of their ideas on their design boards and come up with some stunning color schemes that work very well indeed. You can do the same.

Always remember if you are working with baseboards in another color, you need to wait until the walls are dry so that you don't get paint splashes. If you do the baseboard last, it gives the room real definition that isn't spoiled by splashes of wall paint.

CONCLUSION

Thank you again for downloading this book!

I hope this book was able to inspire you and help you get started on your home makeover project.

The perfect space is just within reach. With a bit of creativity and perseverance, you can turn your boring spaces into works of art that reflect your taste and personality. This book was designed to help you with that goal and working together with the ideas given, you can create a great interior on a budget without having to worry too much about expense. There are ways and means and you will have learned from this book that it's not always about spending. Sometimes, it's just a question of gathering ideas and fitting them into your home space.

FREE BONUS VIDEO: BBC DESIGN RULES 1ST EPISODE: SPACE AND PLANNING

Laurence Llewelyn-Bowen gets right down to the fundamentals of design in this fascinating back-to-basics series. He tackles real problems in real homes as he explores six themes: space, color, light, texture and pattern, balance and order, and personality. In addition to his own in-depth knowledge of design principles, Laurence calls on a color forecaster, psychologists and a perception specialist to explain and demonstrate the science behind the how and the why.

Bonus Video

https://www.youtube.com/watch?v=-WX5UjI8IoA

Printed in Great Britain
by Amazon.co.uk, Ltd.,
Marston Gate.